HANDSWORTH
in days gone by

Sandra Gillott

Published by **Arc Publishing and Print**
166 Knowle Lane, Bents Green, Sheffield S11 9SJ.
t: 07809 172872 w: www.arcbooks.co.uk

DEDICATION

This book is dedicated with lots of love and affection to my granddaughter
Edie Elizabeth Coates.

ACKNOWLEDGEMENTS

I would like to thank all the kind people listed below who have given me valuable personal photographs or

supplied me with information to make this book possible.

Mr Jeff Naylor, Mr Eric Chambers, Mr Tony Holmes, Mr Tony Mottram, Mr Ben Clayton, Mr Len Brookes.

Text copyright 2009 © Sandra Gillott

The rights of Sandra Gillott and her work has been asserted by her in accordance with the
Copyright, Design Patent Act 1988

August 2009

ISBN: 978-1-906722-11-1

Published by Arc Publishing and Print
166 Knowle Lane
Sheffield
S11 9SJ

Telephone 07809 172872

Handsworth in Days Gone By

FORWARD

We the people of Handsworth should be very grateful to previous inhabitants of Handsworth, especially we should be grateful to Mr Sprigg the local newsagent who took many photographs of Handsworth in 1891. Since 1991 I have also taken lots of photographs of Handsworth standing in the same place. Other people who deserve our gratitude are Canon Heneage Ferraby and Florence Earl who both recorded the lives of local people, the buildings and local customs etc.

The Handsworth museum which is based in the Handsworth Parish Centre is full of artefacts, photographs, maps and other items of local interest donated by the people of Handsworth.

On a personal note I would like to thank my husband Keith for his patience over the last few months, also I would like to thank all the people who have given me photographs, to make this book possible.

I hope you get as much pleasure from reading it as I have in compiling it.

Finally I would like to thank the members of the Handsworth Historical Society who have supported me since I became their Chairman in 1992.

Sandra Gillott

August 2009

This white house is the home of Mr & Mrs Arthur Roebuck on Owlergreave Road - now Prince of Wales Road.

The garage and shops at the bottom of Main Road, Darnall, during the 1960's. The Waverley Garage on the right of the photograph is boarded up prior to its demolition, the building at the other end of the terrace is the dentists belonging to Mr Bentall.

These houses and shops now demolished stood on the right side of Main Road, Darnall. They were demolished in the early 1970's.

Miners at "Candle Main" of the Silkstone Seam, near High Hazels Park, Darnall, during the 1912 coal strike. The colliery sign can be seen in the background.

High Hazels Park, Darnall, was officially opened as a park in 1895. It was one of the largest parks in Sheffield and it's beautiful landscaped gardens were classed as the finest in Yorkshire. It also boasted one the best floral clocks, which each year had a different design. During the 1930's it was a very popular place with the boating lake being a major attraction. Whitsuntide parades and sings were also held in the park.

Work starting on the Sheffield Parkway making it into a dual carriageway. The triangular section in the centre of the photograph is the site of the old open air swimming pool. c1980.

Two of the Buxton brothers standing outside "The Elms" on Handsworth Road. The house was the home of another brother Leonard.

Two more Buxton brothers. On the left William 1823-1909 and on the right Joseph 1826-1902.

Moore and Wrights office building on Handsworth Road, it later became James Neill's in August 1996. The buildings were demolished in November 1998. The Asda Hypermarket now occupies the site.

"GLENWOOD" HANDSWORTH.

This postcard is of "Glenwood" on Handsworth Road, it was the home of the Buxton family. In later years it became the Alfred Gold School of Dancing. After the building was demolished flats were built on the site. On the reverse of the postcard the sender has written "This is Sally Bennett's house where she is in service."

Colin Batty a member of the Handsworth Historical Society erecting a blue plaque to commemorate the 300th anniversary of the birth of Benjamin Huntsman in June 2004. Benjamin Huntsman's cottage was situated on the Main Road at Handsworth, and it was whilst living in this cottage he invented crucible steel. The cottage was demolished in the 1920's. New houses were built and the road renamed Handsworth Road. The plaque is situated on the wall of no.189.

Adrian George Mottram the son of Farmer Thomas Mottram stood in the farmyard of Handsworth Hall Farm. Three of the outbuildings of the farm can be seen in the background. Handsworth Hall was built in 1577 as a retreat house by George Talbot, The 6th Earl of Shrewsbury. The hall was turned into two farms. It was demolished in 1969, the Finchwell Estate stands on the site.

One of the Gypsy children who lived at Handsworth Hall Farm. A gypsy caravan stands in the background of the picture. The gypsies came each year to the farm and helped work on the land in Handsworth. Farmer Mottram let them stay in the fields at the side of the farm, and the children were educated at Handsworth School.

This photograph shows Thomas Mottram and his brother in law Jack Buck stood aboard "The Royal Chester" in the bottom cow yard at Handsworth Hall Farm in 1926 . The traction engine was owned by John Earnshaw of Gleadless, who hired out the threshing machine to all the farms in the area. The machine is still known to be in existence.

Bill Scholey, George Mottram and Roy Streeter riding in the horse and trap belonging to G W Mottram of Handsworth Hall Farm. The horse was well known in the area and called "Billy Boy".

Pit ponies outside
Handsworth Colliery.

The Norfolk Hotel in 1903

The rear of Elm House on Handsworth Road, c1920. Extreme right Miss North, George Buxton, Mary Buxton seated, the baby is Frank Buxton.

Handsworth Wesleyan Chapel and Merrill Brothers butchers shop, it was also Carr's Provision Stores, but previously it all belonged to George Roe. Mrs Blunt and Emily Stevenson are stood on the extreme left of the photograph.

The Handsworth Wesleyan Chapel c1920 on Handsworth Road. All the houses and the Chapel lost their front gardens when the trams came to Handsworth and the road was widened.

Girls in Whitsuntide dresses practising their dancing in Handsworth School Yard c1930. The houses on Fitzalan Road can be seen in the background.

Handsworth School Staff c1940's. Back row left to right Joan Singleton, student teacher, Rita Edwards, Monica Smith, Margaret Beech (sec), Margaret Boddy, Ruth Winston. Front row left to right Barbara Staniforth (CCA), Brenda Burton, Miss Dickinson (Head), Louie Braddock, Edith Haynes.

Handsworth County School Junior 1. Class in 1947 outside the boys entrance with the Head master Mr Green and teacher Miss Proctor. Back row left to right Alan Wragg, Brian Harvey, Alan Draper, Brian Bradshaw, Peter Oliver, Edward Harvey, Colin Smith, Brian Robinson, Michael O'Conner, Malcolm Bennett. Second row. John Cowen, Gillian ?, Margaret Schofield, Linda Johnson, Brenda Jones, Beryl Stubbs, Cynthia Hodgson, Elaine Barker, Michael Harris George Shutt. Third row. Maureen Carter, Lesley Heron, Maureen Garside, Mavis Pack, Anne Wallace, Beulah Nixon, Anne Fletcher, Judith Foster, Beryl Swindels. Front row. Keith Nuttall, Michael Gavin, John Dey, Jack Rodgers, Malcolm Rose, Tony Goldstone, David Moss, Michael Holland.

An ariel view of Handsworth, across the top of the photograph is Handsworth Road, with Fitzalan Road to the left. The circular road is Hall Road and St Joseph's Road.

Handsworth Methodists Church parade c1970. Walking along Handsworth Road. The house on the left of the photograph was originally the village carpenters house which had the village mortuary in the cellar.

This drawing by G. Midgley is of the old blacksmiths shop which stood next door to the Turf Tavern. The building was demolished in 1926 to make way for Laverack Street. The tree was known as the Handsworth Oak, and the village pump is to the right.

A tram coming up Handsworth Road in September 1955. The building to the right at the corner of Fitzalan Road is now part of Handsworth Medical Centre with the tall house next door being Manor View.

The New Crown Inn on Handsworth Road, the building to the right hand side is a garage. The sign over the garage says "Tennants Celebrated Ales" good stabling, motor garage and cycle accessories. The sign on the gate advertises the stabling and motor garage.

This sign which states "Handsworth Market"
J T Appleton 1927 stands above the pizza shop
on Handsworth top. The sign is now covered up.

This photograph was taken in 1915, outside the
gazebo which stood in the garden of the "New
Crown Inn". Mr Alfred Wigmore (standing) is the
landlord, with three members of his staff.

The no.770 Ballifield bus standing at the bus stop outside the New Crown Inn, on Handsworth Road, in August 1975.

Mr Garth leading the St Mary's Church parade on Handsworth Road, c1948.

Looking up Bramley Lane c1940. The Plaza cinema is on the left, then the Jeffcock Fountain with Bonds Grocery store in the centre.

Looking down Bramley Lane c1940. The Plaza cinema is on the right of the photograph. This lower door was the entrance to the cheaper seats, which were the front seven rows. Bramley Drive is off to the right and on the left were the allotments, with the large field at the bottom of the lane used for stabling horses.

Mr Herbert Oliver stood outside Bramley Hall in April 1963. This photograph clearly shows the 1922 extension to the hall, with the top two right hand windows and the bottom window was bricked up because of window tax. The stone wall in the front is part of the Ha Ha, which runs around part of the house.

Buxton's Cottages which stood at the top of Richmond Road in 1958, before being demolished in 1960. The Police box on the right was on Handsworth Road. Richmond Road, was previously called Richmond Lane and before that Britton Hill.

A horse and cart belonging to Charles Credland stopping for water at the Jeffcock Fountain in 1920.

Frank Hughes, Chairman of the Handsworth Historical Society with some of the society members at a short ceremony held on July 8th 1988 for the repositioning of the Jeffcock Memorial Fountain on Handsworth Road, after it had been badly damaged by a motor vehicle.

George Shepherd, George Baker and Jeffrey Antony, three of the butchers at the Brightside and Carbrook Co-operative Society Ltd, on Hall Road, Handsworth. The grocery department was adjoining the butchers but their entrance was on Hendon Street just around the corner.

Handsworth Road and the junction of Richmond Road in 1964 before it became a dual carriageway.

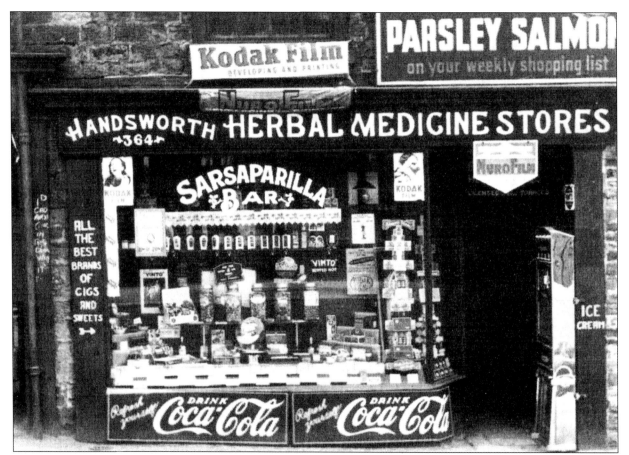

The Handsworth Herbal Medicine Stores, no.364 Handsworth Road. The owner was Mr and Mrs Austin Hughes. The cigarette machine stands in the shop doorway. The shop sign is now in the Handsworth Museum.

The shops on Handsworth Road in 1958. Left to right.
No.364A D & K Mason - Red Circle Library. No.364. Austin Hughes - Herbalist.
No.362 Jeanette - Wool & Drapery. No. 360. Bon Bon Sweets & Drink shop, proprietor Mr Garratt.

The Volunteer Ambulance Drivers on parade on Handsworth Road c1940. The Ambulance Drivers were based at Bowden Houstead Woods. The Handsworth Service Station is in the background of the photograph, all the shops to the right of the garage have been demolished, the site is now an Indian Restaurant and a hand car wash.

Whitsunday church parade May 1953 on Handsworth Road.

Looking along St Joseph's Road towards St Mary's Church c1910. The ivy clad cottage on the left of the photograph was the home of the Scott family. Mr Scott was the village saddler.

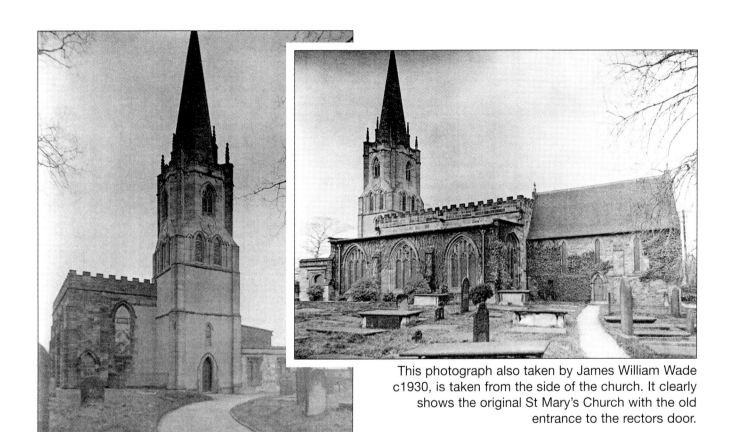

This photograph also taken by James William Wade c1930, is taken from the side of the church. It clearly shows the original St Mary's Church with the old entrance to the rectors door.

This photograph taken by James William Wade is of St Mary's Church Handsworth c1930. The church vestry was not built at the time, and the arch window is visible.

The belfry of St Mary's Church Handsworth. The organ is now in front of the belfry. Before the bell ringers could see and hear the services. The church is decorated for the church flower service.

This royal coat of arms which is hung over the main entrance to the church signifies King William IV 1830 - 1837. It was King Henry VIII who decreed that each church should have a royal coat of arms to signify the link between the church and the state.

Rev. Baker with St Mary's Church Mother's Union outside the parish centre in 1922.

Rev. Baker and Mr Little (church warden) stood outside the parish centre. C1930.

Princess Margaret with Rev Heneage Ferraby at the opening of the Handsworth Parish Youth Wing on 15th November 1966.

A display in the Handsworth parish centre to celebrate the 50th anniversary of V. E. Day on 8th May 1995. A V.E. Day style party was held in the evening with a band and community singing.

Setting up for the St Mary's Summer Fete, July 2001. The building in the background is the Dovecotes. The first mention of the dovecotes was in 1535 when it was recorded that the house, land, dovecotes and gardens were worth 31s 2d. (£1.56).

The Handsworth Sword Dancers, dancing at St Mary's Summer Fete on 24th June 2000.

Cliffe Hill on Handsworth Road. The home of the Jubb family. It has also been a doctors surgery and a residential home for the elderly. It is now a nursery.

No. 534 tram car passing Handsworth Church on 25th June 1956. The tram stop sign on the left of the photograph is now in the Handsworth Museum, which is based in the Handsworth Parish Centre.

The Endowed School on St Joseph's Road. The school was on the left, with the schoolmasters house on the right of the building. The building is now a tyre company.

The Handsworth St Mary's Physical Fitness Class of 1910, outside the Endowed school rooms.

This photograph was taken inside the Endowed School rooms on St Joseph's Road, to celebrate V.J. Day which was the 15th August 1945. The children with their union jacks, lots of sandwiches and buns, while proud parents look on. Note the Japanese model figure in the centre.

The altar and stained glass windows of St Joseph's Church. The Church was built by the Duke of Norfolk and officially opened on June 7th 1881.

Winnie Donlon and Johnnie McGrath c1913.
Winnie was the first May Queen at St Joseph's Church.

St Joseph's Church Football team c1890.

Mrs Mary Barks outside her shop which stood across from the Cross Keys on Handsworth Road in 1922. The signs on the windows state that she was a fish and rabbit salesman. An English and Foreign fruiterer, with wreaths and crosses made to order.

A tram at the Retford Road tram terminus in 1935. Trams started to run to Retford Road on 15th September 1934. Previously they had only run as far as the Norfolk Hotel. Trams ceased finally in Handsworth in May 1957.

The Battle of Orgreave a re-enactment which took place on 17th June 2001. The re-enactment was made up of volunteers and ex miners. This photograph was taken in the field below Orgreave Cemetery, it shows the police getting ready for their famous charge of 1984.

Mr Ben Clayton an ex-miner at the Handsworth Historical Society stall at the re-enactment day of the "Battle of Orgreave" on 17th June 2001.

The entrance to the Asda Supermarket when it was on Rotherham Road. The shop was used in the Oscar winning film "The Full Monty". The store didn't open on Sunday's so the car park was used by learner drivers to practice in.

Orgreave Coking plant, Highfield Lane. 1990.

This miniature portrait is of Peter Cadman (1765-1833) of Ballifield Hall.

The crest of the Cadman family who lived at Ballifield Hall. This photograph is taken from the grave of the Cadman family which is in Handsworth Cemetery.

Ben Clayton, Horace Clayton and Frank Hughes at the Handsworth Historical Society Stall, at the Family History Fair at Sheffield Town Hall.

One of the stones from the Quaker cemetery which stood at the bottom of Grange Lane. The initials on the marker stone are those of William Lord who married Elizabeth Harrison of Orgreave Hall in 1663.

Richmond Lane 1906, now Richmond Road. In the centre of the picture stands a lamp post next to the willow tree which was chopped down to build Laverack Street. As the photograph shows Richmond Lane had a small footpath at each side with a dyke running at the side.

Richmond Road in 1964, the photograph is taken from the same place as the previous photograph.

No.1 Holyoake Avenue in 1920. Holyoake Avenue was named after George Jacob Holyoake (1817 - 1906) who was an avid supporter of the co-operative movement. As the land was owned by Brightside and Carbrook Co-operative Society, it was a fitting tribute to him.

The Skeels family of Richmond Road.

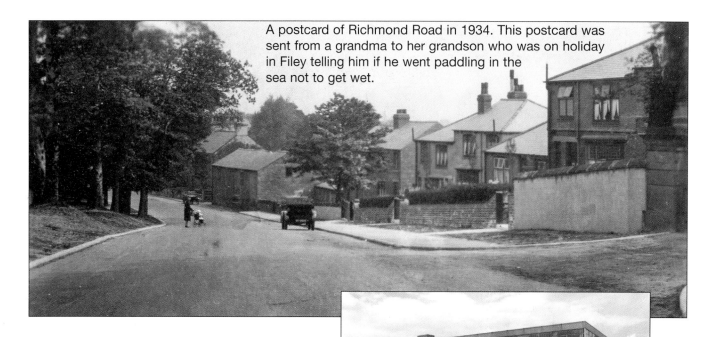

A postcard of Richmond Road in 1934. This postcard was sent from a grandma to her grandson who was on holiday in Filey telling him if he went paddling in the sea not to get wet.

Richmond College which was officially opened in September 1966. The college was greatly extended in 1973 to accommodate the 6,500 students. It became Stradbroke College under the City Council's tertiary review: a further reorganisation saw the building become part of Sheffield College. The College closed down for good in 1997 and was demolished in February 2002. Part of the Highgrove Estate stands on the site.

The Richmond Wesleyan May Queen and her retinue with the children of the Sunday School c1950.

Woodthorpe Hall, a beautiful house built in its own park in 1467 by Henry de Woodthorpe, in the reign of Edward IV. By 1600 the hall was owned by John Nodder, it then passed into the Woodgrove family, then to the Cheney family. In 1736 the most illustrious family, the Parkers came into possession of the hall. John Parker was a Justice of the Peace and Steward of the Sheffield Manor Court. His son Hugh became the first member of Parliament for Sheffield. He was also a member of the Treasury and Admiralty, a Privy Councillor and finally became Lord Darrington. In 1877 the hall was sold to John Bower Brown. It was demolished in 1930. The old Woodthorpe Swimming baths were built on the site and they too were demolished. The park land was used for the building of the Woodthorpe Estate, all that remains is the gate posts on Richmond Road and the fishpond.

The junction of Richmond Road and Woodhouse Road in 1910. This area was known locally as White Rails.

Beaver Hill School Senior Soccer Team
1971-1972. Back row left to right. Dave Smith,
Steve Bryan, Peter Hibbard, Steve Parkin,
David Fuller.
Front Row left to right. Darryl Pitcher,
Kevin Pheasey, Shaun Marsh, Barry Chilton,
Alan Batham, John Wainwright. Paul Webster.

Beaver Hill School U14 Girls Badminton Team
1971-1972 Back row left to right.
Dawn Bennett, Sharon Seaman, Sharon Farmer.
Front row left to right. Josie Howard,
Pamela Maile, Debbie Shaw.

Beaver Hill School Brass Band 1974. The staff members on the photograph include Paul Christian, Cliff Loy, George Holt, John Sharman, Eric Chambers, Des Squire.

Handsworth Rangers Football Club, 1947-1948. Back row left to right Dick Chambers, Arthur Johnson, Brian Sanderson, Frank Vaughan, Jack Leeson, Len Lawson, Bill Armstrong. Front row left to right. Jack Wylie, Bernard Batty, Keith Chapman, Len Brooks (Capt), Frank Gilberthorpe, Terry Vaughan.

Junior 3 class at the newly opened Athelstan School 1954-1955. The children include, David Bellamy, Rodney Vickers, John Britain, Jennifer Watson, Betty Turner, Valerie Kirk, Ann Binney and Keith Lewis.

The Rodgers family of Hall Road.